BADD

Baddy

STEVEN BLYTH

PETERLOO POETS

First published in 1997
by Peterloo Poets
2 Kelly Gardens, Calstock, Cornwall PL18 9SA, U.K.

© 1997 by Steven Blyth

All rights reserved. No part of this publication may be reproduced, stored in a retrieval system, or transmitted, in any form or by any means, electronic, mechanical, photocopying, recording or otherwise without the prior permission in writing of the publisher.

A catalogue record for this book is available from the British Library

ISBN 1-871471-68-0

Printed in Great Britain by
Latimer Trend & Company Ltd, Plymouth

ACKNOWLEDGEMENTS:

Acumen, The Affectionate Punch, Cascando, Envoi, The Independent, Inkshed, Interactions, The North, Poetry Nottingham, The Penniless Press, The Rialto, Scratch, Seam, Smoke, The Spectator, Staple, Tandem, Verse, The Wide Skirt.

"Gig" and "Jobs" have been broadcast on BBC Radio 3.

"First Photo", "Great Aunty Jean" and "Sports Days" have been broadcast on BBC North West radio.

"Story" appeared in *The Long Pale Corridor: Contemporary Poems of Bereavement* edited by Judi Benson and Agneta Falk (Bloodaxe Books, 1996).

"The Storm" won first prize in the 1996 *Staple* Open Poetry Competition.

Some of these poems first appeared in the pamphlet *The Gox* (Redbeck Press, 1996).

Some of these poems were included in a collection for which the author won a Gregory award in 1994.

for my mother and father

Contents

page

9 Sums
10 The Seige
11 Dentistry and Adultery
12 Best Man
13 Hen Night
14 Jobs
15 The Unfinished Obelisk
16 The Gox
18 P is for Poet
19 The Importation of Air
20 Great Aunty Jean
21 The Summer of the Hose-Pipe Ban
22 Gig
24 The Sailor
25 Sports Days
26 Hols
27 Pictures
28 Dave
29 City Tour
30 Baggage
31 Graduation
32 The Robot's Son
33 Summer
34 Pollen
35 Journey
36 Fish
37 In Communicado
38 Karaoke
39 Ugh
40 Questions
42 Visiting Time
43 The Arm
44 Story
45 Pranksters
46 Dorothy

47 The Storm
48 Schooly
49 Baddy
50 First Photo
51 Canteen
52 Highlands
53 Osteoporosis
54 Ghost Story
55 Team Photo

Sums

Here I am, sorting out my belongings
Now me and Sue have split up. Rob is helping.

We load stuff into boxes, then the boot
Of his car. We've agreed that the whole lot

Should be divided straight down the middle.
Rob and me have a rest, put on the kettle

And chat about our friends: Jim and Karen
Who always hold hands, have never been known

To argue; Sally and Peter, who work
Different shifts, rarely meet; Debbie and Mike

With their rows and slamming doors. They all claim
To have found love. I think it's rather strange

But Rob does not. "There are just different ways
Of getting to the same thing," he says

And gives an example: "Fifty plus fifty
Equals one-hundred, and so does eighty

Plus twenty, and ninety plus ten." Later
We find my old school books in a drawer.

Maths is amongst them. It's full of crosses.
They're like the things people put in cards as kisses.

The Seige

I've seen your lover before. A Spartan,
I think. We went to the same school. I'm certain
That he was on my side the day our class
Re-enacted the siege of Troy. Pyrrhus,
That's who I was. Achilles's son. Some desks
Became our wooden horse. Kids who were Greeks
Hid underneath. I went straight for King Priam
When we made our attack. I belted him
With my foil-wrapped ruler and grabbed the queen,
Played by his girlfriend. He had to lie down
Even though he was the school's toughest kid.
No choice. History said he got killed.

Yes, I'm sure of it now: a Spartan soldier.
You walk, hand in hand; I watch from the car,
Wonder whether to drive home, change each lock,
Keep you out, end years of marriage. I think
Things over, staring at the small, red bulb
On the dashboard: the car alarm. My pulse
Doesn't coincide with each flash of the light.
I hold my breath. In a while my heart beat
Will surely change, will match each flash at some point.
I'll never know, of course. I can't hold it
For more than a minute. Today it's icy;
Each breath is a cloud: smoke over a sacked city.

Dentistry and Adultery

My brother and me used to share a room.
His noise woke me one night. I saw him

Trying to hide a telly under his bed.
I knew he'd been on the rob. "Don't you feel bad,

A bit of guilt?" I asked as, shocked, I sprang
From under my sheets. "Course not," he said. "Right, wrong;

Good, bad; sod that. There's no such thing. It's one
Big lie to stop us having fun. It's down

To point of view." Whenever I heard him
After that, I snuggled back into my dream.

I tell her this story when she's feeling
Wicked about our secret and she's losing

Some sleep. I told her it the night before
Her hubby was going to fill my molar.

"I'll have to put your mouth to sleep," he said,
His needle poised. Later that morning I paid

Her a visit. My chin and jaw felt thick
And flabby. It was the anaesthetic

Trying to fool me. I knew they were still lean
And square, the shape she loves. She let me in

And her sexy lips planted a kiss right
On mine. Pity I couldn't feel it.

Best Man

"Bugsy Malone and Al Capone," you said
As we tried on our suits: double-breasted,
Matching, hired from Moss Bros. You started laughing;
I didn't, too worried I'd forget the ring
Or, worse, lose it, and let you down, ruin
My best friend's big day, the friend I'd known
Since I was five: same school, same polytechnic,
Holidays together, a shared bed sit.
I ended up sticking the ring in a box,
The one that used to hold my gold watch,
A box that was too big to lose; I felt
Its reassuring bulk in my pocket.

Now, sitting in your new house, flicking through
Your wedding album, I agree with you
About those suits. Stars of some mobster movie,
That's what we look like, especially me,
So much taller than you, always positioned
Standing at your side or slightly behind,
Just like the loyal minder of "Da Boss",
Like the big bruiser who's always killed off
By some trigger-happy leading character.
It's six months since we last met. In one picture
That box, then still holding the ring, can be seen
As a bulge in my jacket, just like a gun.

Hen Night

The girls have done you up: a big L-plate
Pinned on your back, a bed pan for a hat,
Blown up condoms tied round your waist. They parade
You through the home. "Matron's getting married,"
They tell the residents, "in Spain, on the beach."
They're amazed; in their day the local church
Had to do, then it was off to Blackpool
For a few days. From her wheelchair, Mabel
Asks you to fetch her wedding album. Crippled
By arthritis, she can't even hold
A knife and fork. Hard to believe she was once
The fastest typist in the Coal Board's office.
She met her husband there. He was the bloke
Who fixed the Remingtons when they broke.
Since he died last month, she's written down,
Beneath each snap, the name of the best man,
Each bridesmaid, each guest. You flick through, but find
You can't read them. The names are squiggly lines;
It's the best her stiff, painful hands can do.
They look like foreign coasts she's mapped for you.

Jobs

"I've worked in factories that make these." A fib
My dad used when he was doing repairs
To TVs, fridges, toys. I'd ask if he did,
Really. Mum backed him up. "It's true," she'd swear.

I remember this as I fix the radio
You broke when you chucked it at me. It hit
The wall instead, and you stormed out to go
For Tom, our nephew, who's coming to visit.
Another row: this time about the kid
I want. You don't. "Not yet, not now, next year
Perhaps." You say this every year. I said
It would be good for us, would bring us closer.

When you get back it's working perfectly.
Tom toddles in, grabs my tools, starts to play.
I tell him about the radio factory
I once worked in. "You never did," you say.
Unsure who to believe, a puzzled Tom
Stares at us, frowning, screwdriver in hand,
Like a repair man who can't do the job
Because vital components can't be found.

The Unfinished Obelisk

She's got the sulks, refuses to get off
The coach, won't walk for half a mile to see
"Some stupid chunk of rock." I go by myself,
Fed up of her complaints. She hates this country,

Hates me for bringing her here. "Too hot," she says,
"Bad food. I feel sick. There's too much dust."
We've rowed since we arrived. Our first holiday
Together; it may well be our last.

A guide explains why the ancient Egyptians
Didn't finish this one: "They found the rock
Contained too many flaws. Continuation
Was pointless." He then shows me each huge crack.

Despite these it is still spectacular,
As breathtaking as when I first kissed her.

The Gox

The top of the class in art, that was me,

But bottom in spelling. I used to hate
The way my teacher read out words I'd misspelt.

"Listen. You've put the sounds the wrong way round,"
He'd say. School friends laughed. During the weekend

Their voices swept like brooms through the museum

As they played learning games the staff put on.
I'd sit in the library. I'd shut, then open

My eyes on the pages of the books, my aim
To prove I could see words as just shapes.

I never could. As soon as my eyes opened

Blobs of sound would slap my mind. A small squeak
Came from even the toughest words. Each week

I tried. After an hour or so every time
I'd storm out, go into the museum,

Up to the room full of Egyptian stuff,

Where a sarcophagus lay with its lid
Ajar, a mummy inside. People were awed;

They went silent. It looked just like a huge,
Brown pillow a film's assassin once used

To muffle his victim's screams. Even my friends

Were quiet in that room. I sat and stared
At the hieroglyphics on the side

And lid. They soothed me, the tap of high heels
The only sound in there, like sculptors' chisels.

One summer my grandad came to stay.

"Daft buggers those Egyptians," he said
And pointed at the mummy. "Bloody stupid,

That's what he looks. A bloke who was a prince
Now looks like a sack of spuds. Couldn't face

The fact you rot when you die, couldn't accept

The way things really are." His party piece
Came next: "Open the gox." He threw his voice.

"Gottle of geer." It seemed as though each word
Came from inside the cloth wrappings. I laughed

Loudly. After that I joined in the games.

We made a few rubbings one afternoon,
Did some of a replica Rosetta stone.

There were prizes for the best. Mine came first.

P is for Poet

Numberless, nestled between classes four
And five, makeshift, and once a corridor.

Mrs Davies told us that it was down

To lack of space, but "Thicko! Dummy! Rem!"
Revealed the truth. Words were my biggest problem:

Letters were missing or the wrong way round

In my exercise books, their curls and tails
Like bright kids' arms when they hid answers in tests.

Eight, and still reading books called *blue, green, red,*

With *indigo, magenta* and *violet*
Like foreign place names, tingling like sherbet

On my tongue. Most mornings, we had to read

Aloud. I'd mumble, grunt, or sometimes cough
When I came up against tough words, as if

I had TB, this room like quarantine.

* * *

The English teacher introduces me
To his third years. He's told me I'll probably

Find it most rewarding with the top stream.

He's right; I do. Leaving, I pass the gardener
Trimming hedges, pruning trees. I remember

They said it was parents' night soon. Those blades gleam.

The Importation of Air

Imported air. This was my conclusion,
Standing in the loos at the railway station,
Aged eight. I had just used a hand drier
For the first time. On its side was a sticker.
"Made in the U.S.A." it said.
All that warm air it blew must be collected
Out there, I thought. Perhaps they hung huge sacks
From cacti in the desert to catch
The breeze. After all, such stuff's hard to find
Amongst the UK's icy gales. I reckoned
They flogged it for a fortune over here
To every British hand drier maker.
Whenever I went near one after that
I'd twist the nozzle round. The air hit
My face, blew through my hair. I'd then pretend
I was galloping across prairie land,
A cowboy, roaming the big country, free,
My home in my saddle bags. Yah hoo, ya hee!

One day I got a stetson. Uncle Ted
Brought it back from Texas. I insisted
On wearing it to the shops one afternoon.
A balaclava. That's what my gran
Wanted me to put on. I should have listened
To her. It got knocked off by a gust of wind,
Went under commuter's feet, was crushed flat
As each one dashed back to a semi-detached.

Great Aunty Jean

Her house was neat, like a freshly ironed shirt.
When I went for my tea one of her pies
Was there, perfect and glazed, the table set.
Even when I thought I'd arrived by surprise
One was ready; it was like magic. After
Our tea she'd do the hard crossword in an hour.

No one else I knew could do that, not even
My brainy sister. Once, when off school ill,
I went to stay. "Go out into the garden.
It'll brush the cobwebs away; you'll feel
Better," she said. Outside I picked flowers
For her to press; it was a hobby of hers.

A bully saw me on his way home. "Sick!
More like skiving! I'll tell on you," he said.
She yelled from the doorway, "You do and I'll stick
You one!" He cleared off, never said a word.
After years spent working away, I return
To vist her. A fire in her chip pan

Has blackened the kitchen wall. She hunts for some
Mr Kipling's she swears she bought. Papers
Cover the carpets, their crosswords half done.
I read a clue: *We're only this, all of us.*
Four down, five letters, ending with an N,
Beginning with an H. I pick up a pen

And fill in U M A. "See. I've not lost
My skill at those crosswords," she says. Her chin
Quivers. She stops it by pressing her lips as tight
As her closed cookbook, the one with daisies in.

The Summer of the Hose-Pipe Ban

Last week my dad threw another wobbler
About his garden; it's started to wither,
It seems nothing can be saved. Up in my room
I was flicking through an old family album,
Looking at snaps of my grandma and me
On day trips. In them, I'm about three
And she's always holding my hand; no doubt
To make sure I don't get lost in the crowd,
Separated from her. Alzheimers set in,
So I've been told, soon after they were taken.

Mum wheeled her back from the nursing home later
For our barbecue party. I pushed her
Onto the yellowing lawn, beside the shrubs
That had gone for a Burton. Dad did kebabs,
Burgers, chicken wings, the works. I fed her.
I didn't speak. No point. She can't remember
Who I am, her own name, where she lived. Worse
I can only remember her like this.
That night the first clouds for weeks began to form.
I felt the faint touch of rain on my palm.

Gig

Gig. It's a word she uses all the time.
She goes to lots and tells me about them

After class. Gig. I like its sound, the way

It begins and ends hidden in the back
Of the throat. She's not my best pupil. Her work

Is full of inappropriate words,

And I like to see proper usage. "Roget's,
Fowler's, the OED. Buy them," I say

To all my sixth formers. I've gained respect

Amongst my colleagues as a man who knows
His definitions. Once, she asked if I'd go

To a gig. "It's at the soccer ground," she said.

I would have loved to have gone. But she's young.
What would people think of me? While gardening

I heard them playing. Songs and pop groups

I didn't know. A small aircraft flew over,
Filming it. Now there's a sound that's familiar,

One of the first I remember. I was eight,

It was wartime. We were on a field trip.
Our teacher's voice was drowned. A hit Messerschmitt!

We were hurried away. I hid, had to see.

Slowly, the wreckage's propeller still turned.
The engine chugged. No, that's not right. The sound

Came from deep inside it. More of a gig, gig, gig.

The Sailor

He missed the British rain; that's why he left
The navy. When it tapped on his window
He'd saddle up his horse. "The man's daft,"
People said as he trotted round. He rode
Down to my primary school every day,
Driving other teachers mad, storing sacks
Of feed in classroom cupboards, the squashed grains
Punctuating the pages of text books.

He saved my skin one afternoon. Miss Peel
Asked us to do a picture of a farm.
I painted giraffes and lions in the fields.
Some other kids did cars, clowns, bikes, their mum.
She tore them up. "That's not what I asked for!"
I panicked as she approached my desk.
I faked some tummy pains to distract her,
Curled up on the floor like a question mark.
Someone went to fetch the head. He ran in,
Holding his African bottle. He poured
A cup of its clear liquid for me. "Down
In one. It should do the trick," he said.
Its icy, tasteless trickle unzipped me
And fear walked out, hands raised. "A witch doctor
Gave this to me." We got that story till three
And the home time bell. I left with my picture.

They got him pensioned off; he went to live
With friends in Kenya. He gave me the bottle
Before he left. I'd unstopper it, leave
It on our doorstep overnight in drizzle,
Showers, and thunderstorms. First thing next morning
I'd send the water through the earth to him —
Down the kitchen plughole, the glug, glug, glug
Just like the sound of a rejoicing drum.

Sports Days

What mattered back then? I'll tell you what:
Matter, that's what. The solid stuff: the weight
Of the shot put, the thud of a soccer ball
Against your instep, the crack of a hurdle
Against your toe. That's what counted. No medals
For kids who were good at trig; and girls
Weren't impressed by a grasp of each type of verb
Or meanings of long, scientific words.

He'd try and dodge it, of course. Say he was sick,
Hide in the loos. On the fields we'd make
Life tough for kids like him — swots who were top
In all that airy fairy classroom crap.
He hated matter: boots walloping his shins,
Corkys bowled at his head and, worst, those javelins.

On sports day, they'd take us out to the track
To watch the best compete. He'd lie on his back
And stare at clouds, admire the way they floated,
Weightless. He'd identify the type of cloud,
Then wait for the inevitable rain,
The postponement, being sent back in,
Shouting their names as he ran back to school:
"Nimbostratus! Altocumulus!" Each one
Just like the words of a magical spell.

Hols

Whoppers: The States, China, The West Indies,
Mongolia. And I believed him! Really
He'd spent a week in Carnforth; he did
Every Summer. There, his train mad dad
No doubt dragged him round the Steam Town museum
For hours, standing him on footplates. Next term
He'd come to school full of stories for me
About long haul flights, monkeys' brains for tea,
Trips to the Great Wall or a Ming Tomb,
Knocking for six my fortnight in Benidorm.
Eventually, I sussed the truth, felt stupid
And hurt, and hung around with other kids.

He's not grown out of it. I'm told he's worse
These days. I've seen him several times. Once
From my window seat on the train to Blackpool.
He was reading platform two's time table,
The one on the wall, one I knew for a fact
Was out of date. He turned away from it,
Looked up the line expectantly, for a train
That should have shown up at any minute,
But had long since become a kind of fiction.

Pictures

My colouring was careless. It went over
The lines. My friend's drawing made it happen.
I couldn't keep my eyes off his Eden
And his Eve, who had no fig leaves to cover

Her boobs. He'd even given her hair down there!
Our sunday school teacher tore it up.
She stood him in a corner and said, "Keep
Inside the lines," to me. "God doesn't care.

He's not bothered. I'll bet he's not looking
At our drawings," I said. Then she told me
He was all-seeing. He was sure to see.
"He's everywhere!" Outside, the wind was swirling

Around. I tried to find shelter, but found
I couldn't. It blew her blouse tight, raised her skirt.
It fluttered, looked like scribble. I got a straight
Line in my pants. Something yearned to go beyond.

Dave

"It's hot. Good food. Made lots of mates. Great fun.
Come and visit." That's all his postcard said
About Cairo. Hardly descriptive flair.
Nothing complex, no commas, not one colon
In sight. It seemed she'd been right, our school's head
Of English. She'd point at his empty chair,
Say it was his loss, say he'd never learn
How to express himself with any skill
Or accuracy. He used to tell me
He didn't give a toss. He carried on
Bunking school, working on his brother's stall
Flogging knocked off trainers, jackets, and jeans.

I took up his offer, went to visit.
He was doing voluntary work out there.
I'd been abroad before, but not to a place
Like that. My first day was spent at a market:
So many smells, noises, flashes of colour,
Each one sudden and brief, like a short sentence.

City Tour

The pandas are glum Pierrots;
They're huddled near the shelter's door,
Locked out for us. Tiananmen
Is next. Our guide doesn't mention
Recent events. Why? Someone's theory
Is that it's more than his job's worth. Maybe,
But the smile-lines around his eyes and lips
Seem as accurate as the street maps
We've bought. And there's a sense of pride
When he lists what will fit inside:
"Your Wembley, a liner, two jumbos."
Amazing what this square can swallow.

We visit Mao's mausoleum,
Feel sure he's wax. They've covered him,
From the neck down, in a flag. Plump
And small, he's like a brat tucked up
For the night; it's as if the hundreds
Who pass each day with bowed heads
Are shuffling through a dream he's having,
Are the details that, come morning,
He won't recall. Sobs from the Chinese
Echo, sounding like the cries
Of trapped birds; it is a sadness
That can't migrate. Outside, from us,
Comes the click of Kodaks and Fujis:
The cluck of a different species.

Baggage

When I bunked off, I'd hide books under my bed.
This meant no lugging them round the local
Precinct. I'd leave home with an empty holdall
That never failed to fool my mum and dad.
The first time, I was nervous, sure they'd sussed
My plans. I did it more and more, until
I was hardly ever at school. A doddle!
I'd be with mates, bag swinging round my head.

Amazingly, I passed my mocks. Mum
And dad were pleased, hugged me, so glad I'd worked
For once. At last I'd put my mind to it.
On the first Monday morning of next term
She proudly packed my bag for me. I picked
It up; it felt as heavy as guilt.

Graduation

Mucking about with invisible ink.
Lemon juice was best. When it dried, I'd stick
The sheet over a flame, see what I'd hidden
Emerge. Just one way I'd waste time back then;
Too busy doing that sort of thing
To knuckle down and swot. Instead of listening
My mates and me passed seemingly blank paper
Round class; we revealed their secrets later
With matches as we smoked a sneaky Capstan.
I failed my eleven plus, went on
To get just two O-levels. Bad grades at that
And not ones they reckoned mattered, like Maths
Or English. A-levels next. I flunked the lot
And I knew it. When the results came out
I stayed in bed, each deep sleepy breath
Like the sound of a long drawn out F.
Years later I did a part-time degree,
Juggling day jobs and night school for five years.

Today at work they're calling me brain box,
Clever clogs, prof, Bamber. Everyone shakes
My hand. Unused to this attention
I get embarrassed, feel my face burn,
Look at my shuffling shoes, think " . . . And if policeman C
Has size tens, what size are the feet of policeman D?"

The Robot's Son

She butts in, answers my question perfectly,
Tells us she read it in her dad's books. "Shut up,
Rebecca", her dad, our lecturer, says.
Tonight, his child minder is feeling poorly.
At just twelve his daughter has a good grasp
Of stuff that baffles me every Thursday.

I read sci-fi comics at her age. Dad's
Old collection. I was rotten at reading.
At school my teacher gave comics the blame.
At parents' night, she said, "Make sure he reads
More advanced things". They never did. That evening
Dad got annoyed. "There's nothing wrong with them!
What does she know?" He bought me a comic
On principle the next day. In one story
There was a boy who looked like me. He'd been
Brought up by robots. A load of plastic,
Metal and rubber, that's what his family
Were made of. Unloving, uncaring machines.

It's raining when my evening class ends. Braced
For a soaking, I start to walk home,
Then see my dad waiting in his car. I dash
Across the road, climb in. He says he noticed
The rain. He drove over specially. It's warm
Inside his car. I smell the sweat on his flesh.

Summer

Goose pimply and (despite my mum's advice)

Without a jumper, I'd hug dad for warmth,
One of my cheeks pressed against his paunch,

As we walked back along the seafront

After an evening on the fair. The moon
Was out by then, like the dot at closedown

On the chalet's clapped out TV. Seeing

As it was the holidays, he'd let
Me stay up past my bedtime, watch the late

Movie. I'd glean some swear words, glimpse some breasts.

A brisk handshake is how we touch each other
Now. And this is just at Christmas and New year,

As if on such days some rule is lifted.

Pollen

He'd sit there with a box of Kleenex. Mum
Always had the foresight to pack some
Among the sandwiches. I'd roll down hills
Cut that morning, a little sack of giggles.
He'd never play; foul-tempered, he'd just moan,
Sneezes making summer shiver. At home
Antihistamines kept him drowsy,
Feet up in front of the telly.
If pestered too much he'd raise his hand.

"I'm a winter person," he'd say, and would stand
On touchlines, without a coat or pullover,
While I froze on the wing, too cold to care
About the game, the ball thwacking my back.
"Christ, open your eyes, lad!" Ashamed, he'd slink
Away, avoiding the dads' post-match chat.

Still, there was Autumn. Then, all the hurt
There'd been (and that to come) was forgotten,
As if transferred to bruised apples on our lawn.
I'd help him to collect them, pick the rest
From our two trees. We'd sort them, save the best.
A week later, it was harvest festival.
I'd be sent with packet soups, tinned vegetables.

Journey

It was the first time that I'd heard dad swear.
It had snowed heavily the night before.
With forty miles between us and home
He'd decided to stop at an old farm
That did B and B. As we went in he said,
"Don't forget your pleases and thank yous, lad."
He was always one for politeness, manners.
And swearing was definitely out. My ears
Were often being clipped for it. Spilt tea,
Stubbed toes — those words just blurted out of me.

We hardly spoke that night. Mum wasn't there
To start up a chat. His test match down under
Held no interest for me; he felt the same
About my pocket electronic games.

The next morning, the snow was a foot thick
On the fields and farmyard. Our car got stuck,
Its back wheels spinning, sending up a fountain
Of flakes, like sparks from a firework. That's when
It happened. "Shit, shit, shit!" He told me
To get out, push a bit. Soon we were free,
On clearer roads, snow piled up near the pavement.
Dirty stuff. Grey and brown. Not the pure white
I'd seen earlier. But that didn't matter.
At least now we were moving, getting closer.

Fish

The clown ate a goldfish. it was a slice
Of carrot really, but I pulled my face

And squirmed in my seat like every other kid
In the place. "What's wrong with you?" my friend said.

"If you were hungry enough, you'd eat one."
From then on I wondered if starving children

Sat round their pets' bowls, arguing about
Who got first bite. I couldn't find out

Whether they did or not. When pictures of them
Were broadcast on the news at teatime,

My dad changed channels. Once, when everyone
Was in bed, I crept downstairs to sit alone

And watch the late night news. I stumbled about
In the darkness, heard a smash, slammed on the light.

Goldie was on the floor, her tail flapping
As if she was reaching for her head, trying

To make contact, a ring. I couldn't pick
Her up. I couldn't bear to feel panic

Wriggle in my palm. I didn't put her back
In water. I just shut my eyes and shook.

I feared fish after that, especially those
Piled high on markets, still with lidless eyes.

In Communicado

"So where's communicado?" I was seven
When I asked you, my big brother, that question.
I'd seen a film. "He's incommunicado,"
An actor had said. I reckoned you'd know
Where it was. You knew everything. "Near Spain;
A small island," you said. From then on
You told me tales about the place. I planned
To go and live out there, until a friend
Broke the bad news by showing me a map.
For half an hour I searched the seas of Europe.

This Christmas, after two years down in London,
You visit. We put a big party on
To welcome you. Dad opens that best whisky
He's saved, its smell as sharp as the holly
On our front door. You spend the night answering
Questions about life down there. The next morning
You help me wash up. You dry, stick stuff back
Into our new kitchen cupboards. You ask
Where we put the plates, glasses, cups and pans.
I answer: your guide through uncharted lands.

Karaoke

The house warming party in my first home
Was held on new year's eve, the time when mum

Usually put a bit of a party on.
My friends brought a karaoke machine.

We had a scream, spending the night replacing
Tapes' vocals with our own. Even I sang.

I took the mike and clasped my hands around
The top nervously. "Not there!" yelled a friend.

"Let go or you'll never be heard." Then,
About one, mum piped up, "You've missed Big Ben

On TV and no one's been outside
With some coal. What a farce." Soon after, dad

And mum left in a huff. I ran out
Into the cold and grabbed her arm. "Don't

Go yet," I said, but she got in the car,
Scowling. The windscreen had frosted over

And looked like grandma's cataracts, the clunk
Of the doors like her cassette recorder
When she put in a talking book.

Ugh

"So tell him, with th'occurrents more and less
Which have solicited — the rest is silence." He dies.
                    Hamlet: act five, scene two.

* * * * *

I watch the leading actor hold his breath.
It's always the same — at the flicks, in books,
On the stage. Too often they meet their death
With just a bead of sweat, a few specks

Of ketchup. They mutter something profound,
Then ugh! That's it. But the makers of fiction
Have got it wrong. Usually bowels are opened,
There's vomit, loads of blood, the odd convulsion

And they just groan or scream. It's the drugs or pain
Or both. I work in the infirmary,
So I should know. One week, a writer came

To watch. He wanted to reflect the real
In his work. One night there was a nasty crash.
Lots of victims, messy stuff. We had to deal

With all of them. That's when I found him
On his hands and knees. He'd dropped his pen. It's dumb,

I know (I'd been reading some Bram Stoker)
But I thought he was licking blood off the floor,

Making it as clean as his notebook's pages.

Questions

"Due to bereavement we are closed," the sign
On the shop door reads. I should have guessed when,

The other day, I saw the owner's wife,
That cobwebbed look in her eyes, like those of Wilf,

My dad's best friend, after his son's funeral.
I was there, aged ten. I asked, "Why do people

Have to wear out, go wrong, break, die? Why can't
There be just enough of us: no one snuffs it

And no one's born?" They shrugged, said hush. By phone
I asked my aunt, the family's "brainy one."

Even she didn't have a clue. Today
Some children stand outside the shop. They

Are wondering what bereavement could mean.
Each guess is wrong. "Like beverage," says one.

"A sort of drink." "Someone get me a cup
Of bereavement!" a small girl shouts. "Shut up,"

I say. "Your noise will make the widow upset."
Suddenly a phone box across the street

Starts ringing. It yearns for someone to answer.
"Answer, answer," the kids chant. "Go on mister,

Answer." But I can't. The sound freezes me
To the spot until it stops. I then hurry

Back to the archive office where I work,
Finding things that were made before I could talk

Or was born. We see death certificates
Each day. The words the local registrar puts

In each causes box are long and mysterious.
Myocardial infarction is

A common one. Today, when I get there,
One of my colleagues shows me something rare

Written in a box. It's simply "suicide."
"At last," he laughs, "Something we understand."

Visiting Time

A family meeting at mum's: tea, biscuits
And plans. A rota for giving lifts
To the infirmary, plus what we'll do
When the worst happens, a problem that's due
Within a week or so, his haemorrhage
Being huge. It's all for our great aunt Madge,
Who seems stooped more than ever now
As if that handbag tugs her down,
All her worry and shock coiled up in it.

Monday. My turn. I call for her at six,
Am thanked throughout our brief journey,
Then linked as we approach ward C,
Hurrying past machines that crouch in corners
As if about to pounce. He's lying there,
Only a splinter of his mind left;
His blood's current has swept away the rest.
She tries to salvage some of it with talk
And touch. Each of his long faint breaths is like
A line beneath her words, keeping them straight.

We set off back to her house around eight.
I pop in for tea, promise I'll come round
And sort the blocked guttering this weekend.
The overflowing rain raps on the window
As sharply as a ringed finger. Later, I go,

Leave her to face a different kind of DIY.

The Arm

The amputation to stop the spread
Failed. They gave him, at best, six weeks.
"A goblin sits on my stump," he said.
"It tells lies, makes me reach for books
And things with air. That chaplain is just
The same when he perches on my bed
To preach, promising I'll exist
Afterwards." When I found him dead
The gardener was burning heaps of leaves.
Some caught the breeze and blew away,
Blackened. The chaplain's poor eyes
Stared through his thick glasses. "Today,"
He said later, "I saw ravens.
They flew near the fire in the gardens."

Story

A Book at Bedtime blares from my radio
As I drive home from your funeral. Snow
Is falling, adding rust to the coat hanger
I use as an aerial. It's a reminder
Of you: those left in your wardrobe, all bare,
Their faint jangle when I opened the door.

I've turned the volume up to help me shift
A sense of shame, to try and lose it
At the next twist in the plot. The others kissed
Your lips, brow or cheek in the chapel of rest;
I didn't. I wanted to, believe me,
But years ago I heard a story
About a man who kissed a corpse. His luck
Was rotten after that. I started to think:
The long drive home, bad weather, jack-knifed trucks,
Pile-ups. I thought it best not to risk a kiss.

I pull over to rest, wind down the window,
Open my flask. The voice on the radio
Travels across the night. A condemned church
Stands nearby, its headstones askew. The earth
Is penetrated by sound waves, I've been told.
Sometimes they go so deep they could touch bones.

Pranksters

"Heartless." That's one way I was described.
I'd cracked a joke about the way you died.
People reckoned it was no laughing matter.
Tragic. So young. Victim of some nutter
Doing ninety. On your Kawasaki
You didn't stand a chance, were killed instantly.

I remembered something during your funeral
That made me grin: we'd got drunk in our local
One afternoon. Wandering home, we found
A hearse parked outside a church. We let down
The tyres for a laugh, then ran for it, sprinted
For what seemed like miles, scared we'd been spotted,
Would get caught. I remember stopping to rest,
Being aware of the pounding in my chest.

Dorothy

Vibrations from passing trucks caused a crack
In a pipe under the terrace, some reckoned.
Despite experts' denials, she has stuck
To this theory as strongly as to her faith
And her belief that her youngest, Keith,
Is now "up there", looking down. Her husband

Can talk about it: "I'd just got home. Been
On the night shift. Lit the fire. Boom! Like Frank
Bloody Fosbury, I was. Put me in
A wheelchair for three months." She finds it harder.
It's not the grief, it's just lack of metaphor
Or simile. "The house had collapsed like . . ."

Like what? Cards, matchsticks, paper? All these flimsy
Things to choose from. She can't think of one
That's good enough, her mind feeling as empty
As the sky she woke to that morning, tumbling
From bed, nightdress riding up, revealing
The lot, breeze like a midwife's slap. Her son

(The eldest, Paul) was on nearby streets
Doing his paper round. His loud "Oh Shit!"
Shocked some neighbours as much as the bricks and slates
That were blown through their windows. He helped look
For little Keith, about who she can talk
Easily, has lots of stories. Her favourite

Is about games of pirates on the sofa
When she was knitting, every stitch sending
A light tremor from her arms to her shoulders,
Then down to her hips, the sofa shaking
Gently. "Like a ship", he'd say. She wonders
If he imagined storms approaching, hearing,
From the main road outside, something like thunder.

The Storm

She's gone to the trouble of a gift tag,
Ribbon and bow. He unwraps it carefully,
His hands slow and gentle, each like a tool
He isn't yet skilled with. He reads the back;
She's sure it's by an author that he likes.
It's flowers for her, plus tonight's meal.
Last year they skipped all this, their anniversary
Falling the week after she'd changed the locks.

These are tentative times: when he visits
He asks to come in; they sit in separate
Armchairs; he's leaving by ten. On the doorstep,
Recently, there have been one or two kisses;
The toothpaste on his breath is a strange brand.
He's made promises; she worries, can't help
Thinking of the past breakages: cup, plate,
Window, femur, fingers on both her hands.

Returning home from the restaurant, she'll find
The VCR is on the blink. Lightning
Has lashed out and hit the TV aerial.
It's failed to tape the soaps, the memory wiped
By the surge of power. Its LED
Is flashing like a distress signal.
Miles away, in his bedsit, he'll be breaking
The spine, so she'll think he's had a good read.

Schooly

The gull-speckled pitch was farm land
When I was young. It lies between
The yard and me. This morning it rained;
Now, the sun makes the tarmac gleam

Like a silver platter — a small
Transformation I savour before
You appear, bouncing the net ball.
I listen closely, am aware

Of the silence that lies between
It striking the ground and me hearing
It — like the moment between dreams
And waking, a time when I'm reaching

For you in the empty whirlpool
Of twisted bedding. ". . . each raindrop
Like a tear." I write this to you
In letters (unsent), know full well
This simile's a cliché, plain crap,
Just unforgivable. But true.

Baddy

No boos, no hisses, just a few giggles
From a fat kid in the front row. Promoted
From my bit part: Abanazer for a night,
While Keith's voice recovered. I tried my best
To seem mean, especially in that big scene
In the palace, when the stage lights up
Like the Electricity Board's paint box.
The curtain fell like a sigh of relief.
Backstage I could see the disappointment
In their faces, as clear as cue cards.

I have most days to myself, matinées
Being only twice weekly. I spend them
In coffee shops and pubs, always reading
A play, a biggie, like one by Strindberg,
Ibsen, Chekhov or Beckett. Mostly, though,
It's my old paperback copy of Will's
Complete. I hope people will notice, think,
"Ah yes! He's a Macbeth, a Lear, a Hamlet.
He must be. He looks it." I got a part
In Taggart once. A gangster. Four lines.
They edited me out. And there was mum
Taping every episode, telling her friends.

Now it's late February. Panto over.
It's back to school syllabus stuff. The reason:
Bums on seats and all that. The other night
The leading actors dried, stood there in silence
For a good thirty seconds. That's an age
On stage. I was with them, knew what came next,
Could have whispered. Instead, I kept that line
Inside my head, coiled up as tight as a fist.

First Photo

Dad took it in the hospital. They say
He wouldn't shut up about how I looked
Like him. Same eyes, same nose. Years later, he took
It with him when he went to work away.
Mum sent more, done by photographers. They
Put my tie straight, parted my hair, stood
Me there forever, it seemed. If I was good
Mum promised we'd go to Blackpool for the day.

Her brother, my uncle Ted, tagged along
On those day trips of mine. He loved the rides
As much as me, took me on them all: Waltzer,
Big Wheel, Ghost Train, and in his favourite thing,
The Hall of Mirrors. There, I'd stand by his side,
Stare at our reflections, see my face alter.

Canteen

That January they served me my last mouthfuls
Of roasted, mashed, jacket and boiled spud,
All as sensible (and as hard)
As the third pig's building materials.
That was when they abandoned set meals.
I chose chips from then on, made sure I had
A large helping, so that some could be spared
To buy the company of packed lunch girls.

My diet took its toll. On form portraits
In May, I noticed how my skin gleamed
With grease; hair too. And the acne! Pure ooze.
I gave it back next day, said my parents
Were skint. Truth was, they'd never seen it. Ashamed,
I'd hidden it, safe amongst my Playboys.

Highlands

Taken in the late sixties in Preston
This one shows my mum backstage looking tired
After singing. In his kilt, my great grandad
Is next to her. He was her biggest fan.
After a whisky or two he'd go on
About life in Scotland when he was a lad,
Then sing Loch Lomond: "You take the high road . . ."
He taught me the words and made me join in.

He makes me feel wonderfully foreign,
Removed from drab mill towns, where last weekend
I gave to a busker playing the bagpipes.
He stopped as I passed, shouted "Ta mate!" A Blackburn
Accent. The last air left the bag. Out droned
A low note, like a small car as it stops.

Osteoporosis

The sepia doesn't hide the fact she's ill.
Complications caused by her broken bones
Led to her death; it's as if she were stoned.
Her daughter, my great-grandma, saw it all
And went to church each Sunday without fail,
Praying none of us would get it. When told
Of her tumour, she seemed relieved to know
She wouldn't suffer what she'd seen as a girl.

Now, clearing out great-grandma's clothes, I find
Another snap, a family group. To protect
The image, she's folded it neatly, twice.
It's been unfolded so many times
That when I look at it, it breaks apart
Along the two creases that form a cross.

Ghost Story

He caught a ghost with his instamatic.
He kept it in his top pocket: a pale
Face was floating in one corner. He'd pull
It out at parties, scare us kids with it.
I sussed him out when I started physics
At school. It was a trick of the light, that's all.
I wished I had one. I wanted to thrill
Young cousins, be just like great uncle Vic.

I got it when he died — my chance had come!
But after going to his cremation
I put it in a box, out of sight.
That day I'd seen my nephews at the crem,
All in black. I'd thought of a physics lesson:
How that colour comes from the absence of light.

Team Photo

My dad is near the front, his whites blood-stained.
He wouldn't let his mum touch that shirt
Or those trousers. "Souvenirs," he said. Salt
And cold water would wash it out, she reckoned.
Spectators still mention the day he ruined
His whites. He was in the slips. One run in it.
He caught the ball, even though it hit
His face and burst his nose. Howzat! A legend.

The best I managed was reserve at school.
I never got to play, of course. I'd sit
Beside the pitch, amongst the long grass.
There, my hay fever was terrible.
My nose dribbled onto my top lip.
Sometimes I'd lick it, taste the saltiness.